GENETIC DISEASES AND GENE THERAPIES

CYSTIC FIBROSIS

Richard Spilsbury

rosen publishing's
rosen
central

New York

Published in 2019 by The Rosen Publishing Group, Inc.
29 East 21st Street
New York, NY 10010

Produced for Rosen by Calcium Creative Ltd
Editors for Calcium: Sarah Eason and Kris Hirschmann
Designer: Simon Borrough
Photo researcher: Rachel Blount

Photo credits: Cover: Shutterstock: Andrey Popov: main; Andrii Muzyka: bottom; Ustas7777777: right; Inside: Hill-Rom: The Vest™, Advanced Airway Clearance System - Model 105, from Hill-Rom®: www.hill-rom.co.uk: p. 26; Shutterstock: Acceptphoto: p. 41; Afterclap: p. 10; Alila Medical Media: p. 14; Elnur: p. 34; F8 studio: pp. 31, 47; Juergen Faelchle: p. 18; Iakov Filimonov: p. 44; Garnet Photo: p. 21; Astrid Gast: p. 25; Gopixa: p. 36; In The Light Photography: p. 13; Natee K Jindakum: p. 8; Zivica Kerkez: p. 23; Kateryna Kon: p. 7; Magic Mine: p. 4; Mangostar: p. 27; Pavel L Photo and Video: p. 39; Peefay: p. 32; Tatiana Popova: p. 42; Ranjith Ravindran: p. 38; Helen Sushitskaya: p. 17; TaTae Thailand: p. 16; Thanatphoto: p. 33; Elena Valebnaya: p. 43; VaLiza: p. 29; Wavebreakmedia: p. 11; Sirada Wichitaphornkun: p. 20; Srisakorn Wonglakorn: p. 6; Sherry Yates Young: p. 24; YSK1: p. 28; Wikimedia Commons: Jerry Nick, M.D.: p. 19.

Cataloging-in-Publication Data

Names: Spilsbury, Richard.
Title: Cystic fibrosis / Richard Spilsbury.
Description: New York : Rosen Central, 2019. | Series: Genetic diseases and gene therapies | Includes glossary and index.
Identifiers: LCCN ISBN 9781508182733 (pbk.) | ISBN 9781508182726 (library bound)
Subjects: LCSH: Cystic fibrosis—Juvenile literature.
Classification: LCC RC858.C95 S646 2019 | DDC 616.3'72—dc23

Manufactured in the United States of America

Contents

Chapter 1

What Is Cystic Fibrosis?

Most of us have colds now and then, and our noses and throats feel blocked up. We may cough and wheeze, and might feel a bit short of breath. Occasionally, after eating particular foods, we might feel a bit nauseated or constipated or even lose our appetite. Although these symptoms can be annoying, most of us soon feel better. But people who have cystic fibrosis have many of these symptoms for some or almost all of the time.

Cystic fibrosis is a disorder in which the lungs and digestive system become clogged up so that they do not function properly. When lungs struggle, a person becomes unwell. For example, they take in air less

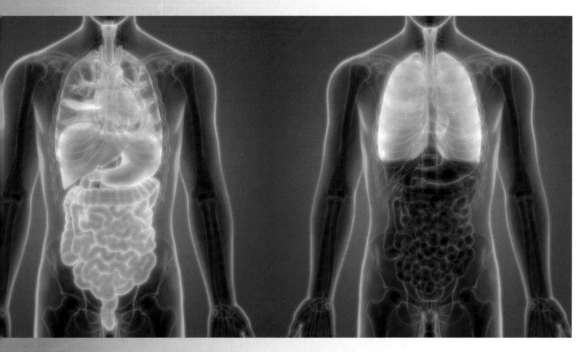

Lungs are large inflatable organs that take up most of the inside of a human's chest. They take in gases from air necessary for respiration and push out waste gases.

efficiently, so they may struggle to get enough oxygen from air into the blood system. This gas is essential for respiration, which is when cells, the building blocks of living things, release energy from food. The digestive system is all about taking in and processing food, on a journey through the mouth, stomach, and intestines. When this system of organs is not working properly, people struggle to get the nutrients they need not only for health but also for respiration. That's why cystic fibrosis has a big impact on the lives of people with the condition.

Inherited Disorder

People get different disorders in many different ways. In many tropical countries, for instance, people need to wear insect repellent to avoid being bitten by mosquitoes. The reason is that mosquitoes can pass on a disease called malaria. People who become very overweight, eat unhealthy foods, and are inactive can develop heart disease. These conditions and many others are acquired from one's environment or behavior.

Other conditions are inherited. This means that people get the disorders from genes passed on from their parents, who got the genes from their parents, and so on. Genes are vital instruction codes, made up of chemicals, that are found in the cells of living things. The instructions tell cells how to grow and survive, what to make that is useful for the body, and many other things. If the genes give wrong instructions, the body may malfunction. This is the case with cystic fibrosis, which is a type of genetic disease.

The Importance of Mucus

To understand the changes that happen in the body when someone has cystic fibrosis, it is important to know about the role of mucus. You probably know this slippery, sticky substance best as snot. When you have a cold, the nose can stream with mucus and you may cough some up. Mucus is vitally important, not only in your nose and other parts of the respiratory system, but also in many other parts of the body.

In the Lungs

Mucus helps to keep our lungs healthy so we can breathe. Air enters the lungs through a network of tubes including the trachea and bronchi. Along with gases, air brings in bits of dirt and dust and also living things such as bacteria and viruses that can cause harm. Cells lining the airways produce mucus that traps any small solid bits, or particles, that we breathe in. To stop the mucus from building up and blocking tubes, tiny structures called cilia on the cells sweep away the mucus and its trapped bits. Cilia are bit like microscopic hairs that move side to side like mini oars. The mucus travels slowly up the airways into the throat. Some mucus gets swallowed and some goes up to the nose, so the body can get rid of it.

Blowing our nose removes mucus that has trapped harmful organisms and dirt that have entered the body.

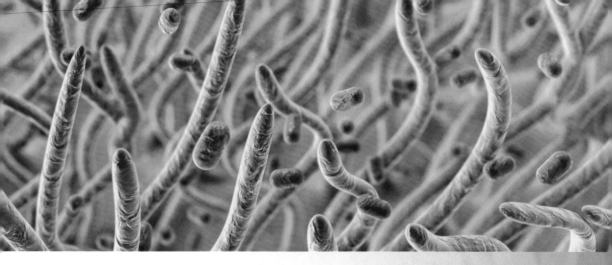

Every minute, tiny cilia lining the airways beat around 1,000 times and move mucus about the length of a fingertip.

In the Digestive System

In the mouth, esophagus, and intestines, mucus has another job: making food slippery so it moves through the digestive system. When we mash up food in our mouths, mucus in saliva (spit) mixes with chopped food to make a slippery paste that's easy to swallow. In the stomach, food is digested by powerful stomach fluids and enzymes from organs such as the pancreas. Mucus from stomach cells is essential in keeping the digestive fluids moving into the stomach and in preventing the stomach from digesting its own walls. Once the partly digested food moves out of the stomach, mucus in the intestines keeps it moving until it is fully digested, then eliminated when we go to the bathroom.

Mucus Change

People with cystic fibrosis have cells that produce lots of thick, sticky mucus. This is a result of a problem with a protein in their cells that controls the flow of water and salts in and out. When the protein does not work properly, salts get blocked and mucus is made with less water in it, so it is thicker. With thicker mucus, cilia in lungs cannot work as well, meaning that airways can get clogged easily. Infections can happen when bacteria and viruses get trapped in the airways. Instead of protecting the digestive system, mucus clogs and blocks its normal functions.

Symptoms

People with cystic fibrosis experience a wide range of symptoms associated with the disorder. The symptoms typically start to be noticeable in early childhood. Some people develop the first symptoms as soon as they are born, whereas others don't notice them until they are adults. Symptoms can get better or worse with age.

Chest Infections

People with cystic fibrosis have frequent, often long-lasting bacterial and viral chest infections. As a result, they often feel poorly and have persistent coughs and stuffy noses. People with the condition often wheeze when breathing, especially during exercise when the body needs to take in more air.

People with cystic fibrosis often experience lung infections and difficulty breathing. Inhaling certain medications or pure oxygen can ease these symptoms.

Pancreatic Problems

Tubes from the pancreas become blocked so the pancreas cannot release its digestive enzymes into the stomach. This buildup of enzymes can cause pancreatic infections and scarring that can reduce the pancreas's ability to make insulin. Insulin regulates the blood's sugar level. People who cannot regulate sugar with their own insulin are diabetic. Around 50 percent of adults with cystic fibrosis are diabetic, too.

Digestive Problems

A person with cystic fibrosis may have a poor appetite and struggle to gain weight as a result of their body's inability to properly digest and release nutrients from their food. Digesting fatty foods is particularly difficult. This is a reason why people with cystic fibrosis often produce greasy, foul-smelling stools (solid waste). Other digestive symptoms include a swollen abdomen (belly), nausea, diarrhea, and constipation.

Nose and Sinus Problems

Many people with cystic fibrosis have nasal polyps. These are soft growths in their noses that can cause nasal congestion, pain, or loss of smell. The polyps form as a result of blocked airways and infections. Sinuses are air-filled spaces in our skulls between the eyes that help warm and moisten the air we breathe in. People with cystic fibrosis get clogged sinuses due to a buildup of mucus, which can cause pain.

Salty Sweat

If you have ever tasted your sweat, then you know it is a bit salty. Sweat cools animals down, because liquid uses up heat energy from skin to evaporate, or change from a liquid to a gas form. Sweating also gets rid of unwanted salts. Cells in people with cystic fibrosis cannot move salts properly, so they end up needing to get rid of more. The result is very salty sweat.

Chapter 2

How Is Cystic Fibrosis Inherited?

Inheriting something means having traits passed down to you by your parents. When your parents got together and had you, you inherited a blend of the genes in the cells of their bodies. People can only get cystic fibrosis if they inherit the genes that cause it from their parents.

About Genes

Many people would say the things they inherit from their parents are, for example, hair or eye color, being tall or short, or the ability to roll their tongue. The job of genes is to store coded instructions that tell cells and organs to make proteins that affect everything from the color of your hair to how you grow and your health. Remarkably, every cell in a human body contains a complete set of these genetic instructions, stored in the chromosomes in the nucleus, or center, of each cell.

DNA is twisted to pack more coding into a small space. If the DNA in one cell were stretched out, it would be around 6 feet (1.8 m) long!

Humans have twenty-three pairs of chromosomes. Each one is an X-shaped object made up of a special chemical called DNA. Up very close, DNA looks a little bit like a twisted ladder with rungs containing sequences of chemicals. In total, a set of human chromosomes contains around three billion chemicals. We can think of a chromosome a bit like a volume of an encyclopedia with thousands of entries or topics made up of billions of letters. Each gene is like a different topic.

Reproduction and Differences

Each pair of chromosomes is made up of one copy of a chromosome from the mother and one from the father. Male sperm and female eggs each contain just one copy of each chromosome, or just twenty-three chromosomes in total. During sexual reproduction, a sperm fertilizes, or joins with, an egg cell and the chromosomes from each combine to make pairs. The embryo that develops from the fertilized egg contains twenty-three pairs of chromosomes, or two copies of each encyclopedia of genes.

No two people, not even identical twins, are exactly alike. Our differences are due to very slight variations in the genetic code, a bit like small spelling changes, rewordings, or text rearrangements in the encyclopedias. Usually when genes or the proteins they make differ, individuals may look different but the genes and proteins work correctly, so there is no impact on health. However, the genetic changes sometimes have a big impact on health, as is the case with cystic fibrosis.

Many traits, including the tendency to develop a certain disease or disorder, are passed down by a person's parents.

Genetic Mutations

You probably think of the word "mutated" as meaning something artificially changed and gone wrong. In fact, mutations are a normal part of the way genes and chromosomes slightly change over time.

Good and Bad Mutations

Some mutations can be beneficial to individuals and even to whole animal species. For example, in the distant past, some giraffe relatives had gene mutations that made their necks extra long. This trait enabled them to reach the leaves of tall trees. They could get more to eat, so they were more likely to survive than giraffes with shorter necks. They passed that gene to their descendants. Over time, the species changed until all giraffes were born with long necks.

But not all mutations are helpful. Some are bad. In people with cystic fibrosis, mutations in a gene disrupt the normal production and functioning of a protein found in cells in the lungs, digestive system, and other body parts.

Two, Not One

More than 10 million Americans carry a mutation in the cystic fibrosis gene but do not have the disease. This is the case because these people have only one copy of the mutation. People only have cystic fibrosis if they inherit two copies of the mutation—one from each parent.

How does this work? Cystic fibrosis is a recessive disorder. That means that in people with mixed genes, the activity of the healthy copy masks the activity of the faulty copy. So these people produce normal mucus, have fewer lung infections, and so on. They are said to be cystic fibrosis carriers, but they do not actually suffer from the disorder.

The situation would be different if cystic fibrosis was a dominant mutation. Dominant mutations are expressed when there is only one copy in a chromosome. For example, people have brown eyes if they have one brown mutation of the eye color gene, because this mutation is dominant over other eye colors.

Children can inherit either normal or mutated genes from their parents. Whether a gene is expressed (causes a characteristic to appear) depends on many factors.

What Are the Chances?

Doctors talk about the percent chance of children inheriting disorders such as cystic fibrosis. Each individual baby has the same chance of inheriting cystic fibrosis mutations from both parents, regardless of whether his or her siblings have it.

Child of two carriers of the mutated cystic fibrosis gene:

- One in four, or 25 percent, chance that the child will not be a carrier

- One in four, or 25 percent, chance that the child will have cystic fibrosis

- Two in four, or 50 percent, chance that the child will be a carrier

Child of two people, one with cystic fibrosis and the other a carrier:

- Two in four, or 50 percent, chance that the child will be a carrier

- Two in four, or 50 percent, chance that the child will have cystic fibrosis

The Cystic Fibrosis Gene

The gene responsible for cystic fibrosis is formally named cystic fibrosis transmembrane conductance regulator, or CFTR for short. CFTR is a part of the long arm of chromosome 7 in humans, which is just one of twenty-three different chromosomes in the human genome.

The CFTR gene contains instructions to make a wiggly protein called CFTR made up of nearly fifteen hundred amino acids. One job of this protein is to create special gates in certain cell walls that control how much salt and water are let through. Such gates are found in cells

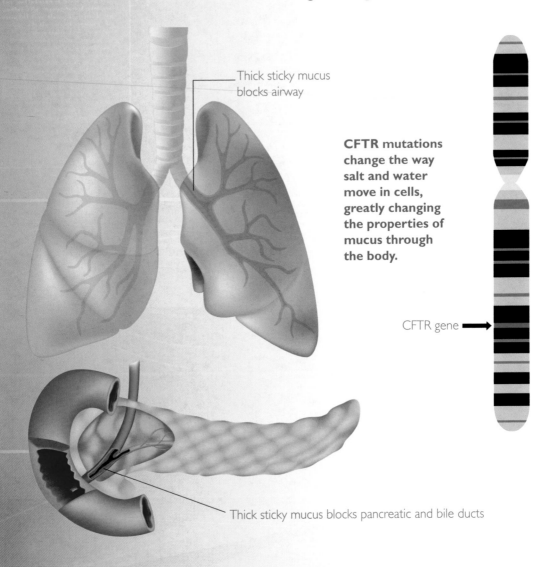

Thick sticky mucus blocks airway

CFTR mutations change the way salt and water move in cells, greatly changing the properties of mucus through the body.

CFTR gene ➡

Thick sticky mucus blocks pancreatic and bile ducts

that make mucus, saliva, sweat, tears, and digestive enzymes. The CFTR protein also regulates other channels in cells whose proper functioning is important for normal function of the pancreas and lungs.

Many Variants

Scientists know that it is not just one type of mutation in CFTR causing the symptoms of cystic fibrosis. There are well over seventeen hundred different variants, or mutations, of the CFTR gene. However, nearly all cases of the disorder in the United States and two-thirds of cases worldwide are caused by a single variant called ΔF508. In this mutation, a slip-up of just three code letters in the gene cause CFTR proteins to be produced by cells that lack just one amino acid. This fault is enough to prevent the protein from working properly.

Different variants and combinations of variants can cause different disease symptoms. For example, people with some variants are more likely to have pancreatic problems, whereas those with other variants often have more lung problems. Still other variants in CFTR seem to have no effect on health and so do not cause cystic fibrosis. Not all patients with the same variants have the same symptoms, partly because other genes affect the disease. For example, mutations in a gene called mannan-binding lectin can make bacterial lung infections in people with cystic fibrosis more likely, no matter what CFTR variant they have.

Gene Genies

Scientists have various theories about how cystic fibrosis first appeared in humans. The mutation in Delta F508 is estimated to be up to fifty-two thousand years old. It is probable that individuals with one copy of this mutation were better able to survive potentially lethal (deadly) diseases such as cholera, typhoid, and tuberculosis. For example, the harmful bacteria causing typhoid cannot get into intestinal (gut) cells, where it causes damage, through abnormal CFTR proteins.

Chapter 3

Diagnosing Cystic Fibrosis

Diagnosis of cystic fibrosis can happen at any age when symptoms arise. However, two-thirds of people with the disorder are diagnosed below one year of age. These diagnoses often result from routine newborn checkups. Early screening is important because even babies that seem healthy may have serious medical disorders, such as cystic fibrosis.

Heel Stick

In one test, a doctor, nurse, or midwife collects a baby's blood sample. The baby is kept warm and its sock is removed. Then the baby's heel is pricked with a lancet, which is a plastic pen-like object with a button that makes a narrow, sharp blade come out from inside and retract again.

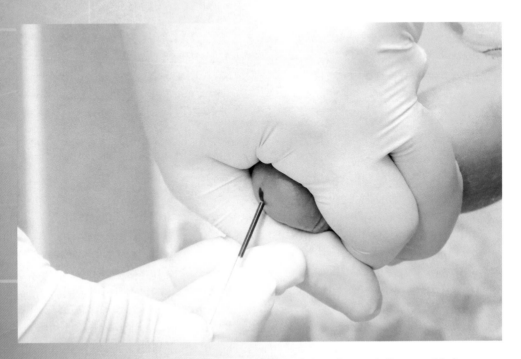

A heel stick can look alarming, but it is virtually painless for an infant, and it is an important part of the newborn health screening process.

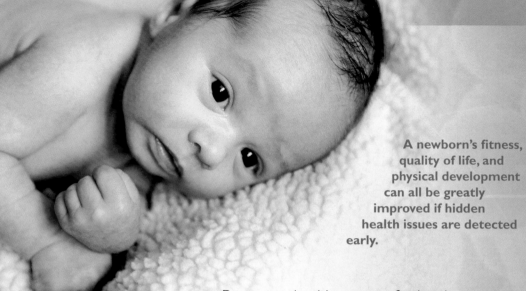

A newborn's fitness, quality of life, and physical development can all be greatly improved if hidden health issues are detected early.

Parents or health care professionals usually cuddle or feed the baby while the heel stick is performed, to help distract and calm the baby. The heel is pressed gently to produce drops of blood that are collected on a screening card to create several dried blood spots. This card, including details of the baby's name, age, and parents, is then sent to a laboratory. Laboratory workers analyze the blood by seeing how bacteria grow on dishes of jelly when a blood spot is added. If the blood contains certain proteins indicating diseases such as cystic fibrosis, the bacteria grow better.

Newborn babies with cystic fibrosis have blood containing higher-than-normal amounts of a protein called trypsinogen. Trypsinogen is used to help make pancreatic enzymes, so if the pancreas is partly blocked, less of the trypsinogen will have been used up. If levels are high, there is a strong chance a baby has the disorder.

Sweat Testing

Sweat testing for raised salt levels is a more reliable method than blood testing, as some people can have raised trypsinogen even when they do not have cystic fibrosis. In the sweat test, a chemical is rubbed onto a small area of an arm or leg. Electrical stimulation is applied for around five minutes to encourage the sweat glands to produce sweat. A person may feel tingling in the area, or a feeling of warmth. The sweat is collected, then tested in a laboratory for its saltiness.

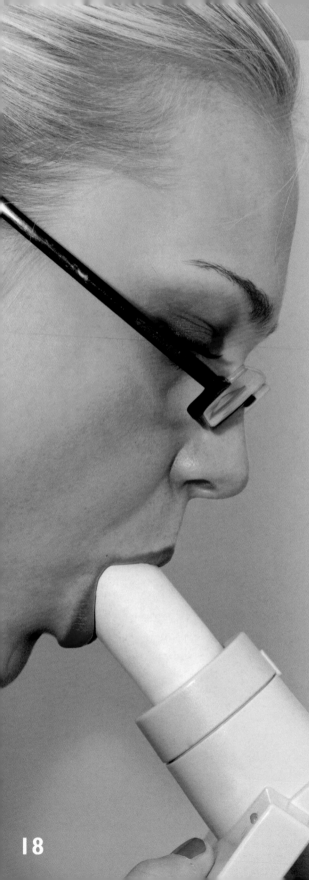

Seeing the Signs

When people feel unwell, doctors check signs of health such as temperature and pulse rate, but they also look out for signs of different diseases or disorders. People with cystic fibrosis often have a medical history of repeated respiratory and digestive problems. If a doctor notices this pattern, he or she may carry out tests that help confirm this possible diagnosis.

Breathing Test

Doctors may use a spirometer to help confirm cystic fibrosis. This electronic device has a breathing tube. A patient breathes in fully before pressing the lips around the mouthpiece on the tube and exhaling as hard and fully as possible. The spirometer measures how much air the patient can exhale in one second and the total amount exhaled in one forced breath. Doctors compare these measurements against normal measurements for someone of similar height, age, weight, and sex. People with cystic fibrosis may have measurements just one-half to one-third of normal spirometer readings.

Spirometers help doctors determine a patient's lung health and breathing abilities.

Clubbed fingers have swollen fingertips and upward-curved nails. This is a classic sign of cystic fibrosis as well as other disorders in which the lungs are struggling to get enough oxygen to the body.

Stool Sample

Wearing protective gloves, patients collect a sample of their stool (solid waste) from the toilet and put it into a sample tube. This sample is then tested in a laboratory for levels of enzymes made by the pancreas, including elastase. If levels are unusually low in stools, it is a sign that low levels are present in the intestine, and that the pancreas could be blocked. Cystic fibrosis is a common reason why this can happen. It is also one explanation for higher-than-normal amounts of fat in stools, although this can also be caused by eating lots of fatty foods.

Imaging

Health care professionals can use a range of different equipment in hospitals to help diagnose and evaluate the symptoms and health care needs of people with cystic fibrosis. Two of the tests rely on X-rays. These are a form of invisible, high-energy radiation that can pass through soft body parts such as skin and muscle.

Seeing Inside

As an X-ray passes through a body, some of its energy is absorbed. Hard tissues such as bone absorb more energy than soft tissues or empty spaces. Machines can detect the pattern of X-rays before and after the passage to produce images of a patient's insides. X-ray imaging is important for seeing inside the lungs of patients with cystic fibrosis to discover what damage the thickened mucus is having on the lungs' function.

Chest X-rays use a beam of X-rays from a fixed position. This exam produces images clear enough for specially trained health workers called radiographers to spot mucus buildup in airways. They can also see any signs of changed tissue in the walls of the lungs that could indicate a lung infection. Then doctors might prescribe antibiotics, which are medicines that treat certain infections. CT (computed

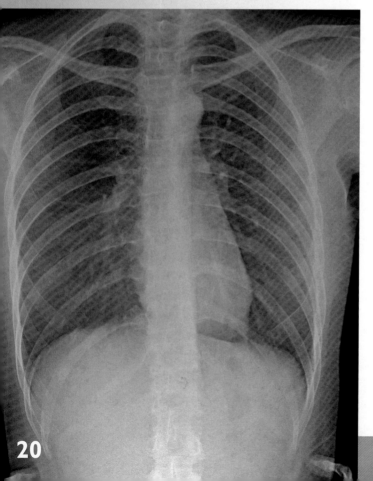

This X-ray shows internal structures, such as bones and faint radiating airways.

tomography) scans expose a patient to weaker X-rays from a source moving around the patient. The patient lies down and his or her bed is slowly transported through a ring containing the X-ray equipment. Imaging by CT provides more detailed and higher-definition three-dimensional imaging. It can show the lungs, the intestines, and even blocked sinuses and polyps in the nose.

Seeing with Sound

Ultrasound imaging uses high-frequency sound rather than X-rays to help diagnose problems. Machinery fires pulses of ultrasound into a patient and "listens" for echoes bouncing back from the insides. It then translates the echoes into images. Ultrasound imaging is ideal for spotting blockages in the pancreas, liver, and gallbladder, organs whose functions are all affected by cystic fibrosis.

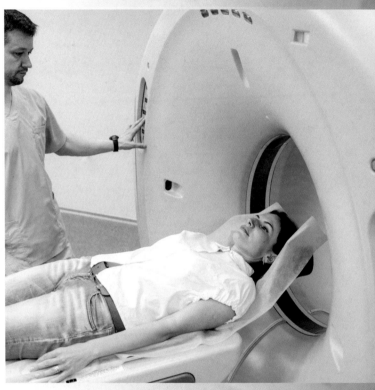

CT scanners produce detailed three-dimensional images of a person's inner body.

This imaging technique is also used to confirm a fairly rare condition called meconium ileus in newborn babies. Meconium ileus is when fecal matter (solid waste) called meconium in the newborn's intestines is extra thick and blocks the intestines, causing discomfort. Sometimes the meconium can twist the bowel and, in rare cases, cause it to split open. Most babies with this condition have cystic fibrosis.

Genetic Testing

Positive heel stick and sweat tests, poor spirometry performance, and problematic stool samples can all lead to a probable diagnosis of cystic fibrosis. The results of X-rays, CT scans, and ultrasounds can make the diagnosis almost certain. However, another way to confirm a diagnosis is through genetic testing. Health care providers order a genetic test for people suspected to have cystic fibrosis, based on other tests and signs, for two reasons. First, it can confirm whether they have a mutated CFTR gene or not. Second, it can also identify which variant they have.

Cells for Testing

Laboratory workers can analyze cells from heel stick testing and other blood tests, and cells from other sites around the body. One of the easiest places to get these cells is the mouth. Cells inside the cheek help protect the underlying tissue from being worn down, and from damage by heat and chemicals in food, by forming a loose layer of dead cells. Health care workers may rub a swab gently around the inside of a person's mouth to pick up cheek cells. Patients may also swish a special mouthwash around to wash away cheek cells. The swab or mouthwash is collected and the cells they contain are sent to laboratories for gene testing.

Reading Genes

The first step in reading genes is to get DNA from inside cells. Cells are put into a special detergent that splits them open by destroying membranes around the cell and nucleus. Other chemicals digest away proteins and separate the DNA from the mix. Technicians then use special techniques called DNA sequencing to read the genes in the DNA. These involve using ultrasound to break the DNA into shorter pieces. They are then treated with heat and different chemicals so computers can read the sequences of chemical codes in the genetic material. Any mutations in CFTR can be found through DNA sequencing.

Cells for genetic testing can be collected by rubbing a swab on the inner cheek.

Early Testing

Carriers of the cystic fibrosis gene often want to know if their unborn child will have the disease or just be a carrier, so they will be ready to deal with the symptoms and issues as soon as the baby is born. That is why genetic tests are also performed on cells in amniotic fluid, which is the fluid that surrounds a fetus during pregnancy. The procedure to take amniotic fluid, or even cells from the umbilical cord, has to be done very carefully to avoid any possible harm to the baby or mother.

Chapter 4

Treating Cystic Fibrosis

People with cystic fibrosis have a wide range of treatment options that can improve their day-to-day lives, help them deal with the more serious health problems, and reduce the chance of having severe symptoms.

Drug Therapy

The struggling airways and lungs of people with cystic fibrosis can get some help from a wide range of different medications.

Antibiotics: These are medications that kill bacteria or prevent them from reproducing or spreading. They do not work against viral infections. People with cystic fibrosis take antibiotics such as azithromycin, usually in pill form, several times per week. These medications prevent bacterial infections and airway inflammation (swelling).

Mucus busters: Some medications help to break down thick mucus so it is easier to cough up. For example, an enzyme called DNase dissolves leftover, springy DNA from dead cells in the lungs and thins the mucus in these areas. Other drugs thin the mucus by changing the balance of salt in airway cells so they suck in less water from the mucus.

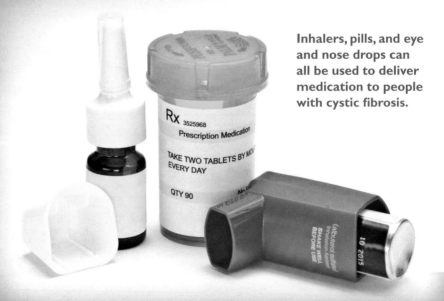

Inhalers, pills, and eye and nose drops can all be used to deliver medication to people with cystic fibrosis.

Widening airways: Bronchodilators such as albuterol relax muscles in the airways to increase airflow to the lungs.

Surgical Treatment

Scarring and infections over time can leave some people's lungs in a very poor state. They may be so damaged that they can only manage 30 percent of their normal function. In these cases, a lung transplant is considered. This can only happen if an appropriate donor has recently died and has put their organs up for donation to the sick. Lungs need to be a match in size, age, and other factors to make a transplant most effective. There is a shortage of donor lungs, but for the lucky recipients, new healthy lungs can transform their health.

Organ donors offer a lifeline to people struggling with cystic fibrosis and many other diseases.

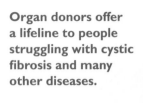

GENE STORIES

"Just a year ago, life was very difficult. I needed to wear an oxygen mask 24/7 for my poor lungs to work at all and I was so weak I had to move in a wheelchair. It was a shock when the new lungs finally arrived from the donor, because you never know when it might happen, and the idea of the operation and recovery was scary. But I cannot express how happy I am that I had the transplant. Now I can bicycle, go to the beach, and live a pretty normal life. Thank you, donor, for saving my life!"

—Jasmine, age sixteen

Physical Therapy

One of the most important ways to make sure people with cystic fibrosis feel as healthy as possible is to use physical therapy. The main objective of physical therapy is airway clearance, or getting rid of mucus buildup.

Airway Clearance

There are many techniques for airway clearance, and people with cystic fibrosis typically do them one to four times every day.

Percussion: A person leans forward while someone, such as a relative or a health care worker, claps cupped hands along the sides of the chest. The cupped shape captures air that softens the blow. Like beating a drum, percussion is done with a steady beat. The blows loosen the sticky mucus in smaller airways. Vibration with a flat hand on the chest gently shakes the mucus into larger airways.

Breathing techniques: Physical therapists can teach controlled breathing in different parts of the lungs to clear them. Deep breathing is sometimes combined with huffing, coughing, and relaxed breathing to move mucus along.

Physical therapy machines: A high-frequency oscillation vest is a device that inflates and vibrates at high speed to push against the chest and help shift mucus from it. The vest mimics percussion

Percussion vests vibrate to loosen mucus within the chest and shift it into large airways, where it can be coughed up.

activities. Some other machines have masks that patients wear to develop stronger exhalation, which can help clear airways.

Treating Incontinence

Incontinence is when people accidentally leak some urine or release feces. This is embarrassing but not unusual. It happens in around one in seven women in the United States. Urinary incontinence can be triggered by coughing or sneezing, which make abdominal muscles contract strongly and push on the bladder. If the pelvic floor muscles fail to keep the bladder closed, urine leaks out. Women with cystic fibrosis cough much more and much longer than usual, so they may have specialist physical therapy to learn "the knack." This is an exercise that involves tightening and lifting the pelvic floor muscles before coughing to protect against leaks.

GENE STORIES

"My normal airway routine starts early each morning on school days. At 6:00 a.m. I put on my percussion vest for about forty-five minutes while I read, check messages, or catch some morning TV. The vest really helps to loosen the gunk that built up overnight. I puff on my inhaler to help relax my airways and then comes the unpleasant part of the day: coughing over a bowl!"

—*Shona, age seventeen*

Exercises to strengthen core muscles in the body, including the muscles of the pelvic floor, can help people manage some cystic fibrosis symptoms.

Diet and Exercise

Medication and physical therapy are important ways to deal with the symptoms of cystic fibrosis. However, like all people, those with the disorder can help their general health by being careful about what they eat and doing lots of exercise.

Helping the Digestive System

Only about 10 percent of people with cystic fibrosis have a pancreas that can produce enough enzymes to digest their food properly. The rest cannot naturally get enough enzymes into their digestive system, so they take enzyme capsules with every meal and snack. People with cystic fibrosis often cannot digest and absorb fat and protein properly, so they have to eat a higher fat and protein diet than people without the disorder.

Health care professionals called dieticians also advise people with cystic fibrosis to eat twice as much food as people without the disorder. This is because people with cystic fibrosis need to take in more energy to help them fight chest infections and build up their energy reserves to cope with weight loss during the frequent episodes of illness that they have. High fiber diets, with plenty of vegetables and whole grain bread or pasta, can also help reduce the symptoms of constipation and diarrhea.

A diet rich in fresh vegetables, beans, and fruit can improve anyone's health, not just those with cystic fibrosis.

Staying Active

Exercise really helps people with cystic fibrosis. It helps to keep the body fit and healthy so it can cope better with the condition. Exercises such as running, swimming, football, or tennis that make people feel out of breath are especially good. These help to keep the lungs strong so they are better able to clear mucus.

It's also important for people who have cystic fibrosis to keep their chests and shoulders flexible and relaxed, so they don't tighten up and make symptoms worse. Physical therapists can show adults simple stretching exercises that can help to keep all these muscles flexible. Younger children can be encouraged to play games that involve lots of moving and stretching of the upper part of their body and arms.

Drinking plenty of water is important for everyone, especially when exercising, because we lose water when we sweat. But drinking water helps people with cystic fibrosis in other ways, too. Water helps to thin the mucus in the lungs, which makes it easier to get rid of it.

Chapter 5

Living with Cystic Fibrosis

Everyone with cystic fibrosis is an individual with his or her own version of the disorder and a unique range of symptoms. With advances in treatments, cystic fibrosis is no longer as limiting to people's lives as it was in the past. But for most people, it still affects their day-to-day lives in different ways.

Ups and Downs

When people are well, having cystic fibrosis doesn't stop them from doing everything they want to do. However, when they are unwell, it can take several weeks to get back to normal. This can be difficult. For example, when people get infections they may be in and out of the hospital until they are better. They miss work and school days, which means they fall behind. When this happens, people can help themselves by planning something enjoyable for when they leave the hospital or feel well again. Having something positive to look forward to can help them through the bad times.

Taking Time

Dealing with cystic fibrosis can also take a lot of time and effort in a person's day. Just taking all of the necessary medicines can take time. Some people with cystic fibrosis need to swallow fifty or even sixty pills every day. They may also have to use an inhaler or have other treatments, too. On top of that, they may have to make time to do one or two hours of physical therapy or stretching exercises. Even just eating the extra food they need to have every day can be a chore. This is especially true for young children who would rather be playing and don't understand why they have to eat more and more. The treatments and condition can be very tiring, and that can make it hard for people to cope with their everyday lives sometimes.

People with cystic fibrosis have to take a lot of medication, but it is important. It helps them feel well enough to get on with their lives.

GENE STORIES

"I was twelve years old when I learned how to do my exercises properly and take my medicines by myself. My dad taught me how to do it. It's good to learn to do your own treatments and take care of yourself. It makes me feel more independent and happy now that I'm not relying on somebody else all the time. It's my body, so it's important that I know how to look after it. Everyone should know how to take care of themselves!"

—*Chris, age fourteen*

Taking Care

As well as taking their medications, having physical therapy treatments, eating well, and exercising often, people with cystic fibrosis also have to take care of themselves in other ways.

Avoiding Irritants

Cystic fibrosis sufferers have to avoid anything that might cause them to make more mucus, because this will make their symptoms much worse. This has a surprising impact on their lives. For example, people with cystic fibrosis who have long hair never leave their hair wet, because the cold and damp would make their lungs produce more mucus. All sufferers must avoid mold, smoke, and pollen because these substances are irritants as well. This means they have to be careful when they go outdoors, because mold is often found on plants, soil, or rotting vegetable matter, and pollen is a powder released by flowers and trees in summer.

Avoiding Infections

People with cystic fibrosis are at greater risk of getting lung infections than other people. When mucus builds up in their lungs, bacteria thrive

Hand washing is a simple but effective way to eliminate germs, and give airways a helping hand.

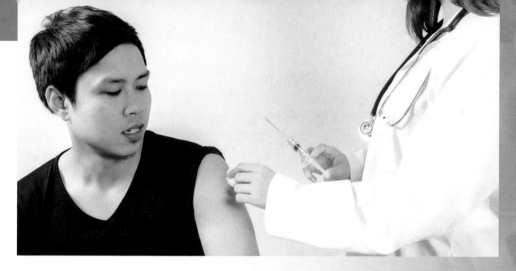

If people with cystic fibrosis get the flu, it can lead to a severe lung infection. So they get a flu shot each year to help them avoid it.

and multiply. So these people always have to try to avoid germs. For example, many germs are passed on by dirty hands. When we touch an object such as a doorknob that someone with an infection has touched, then we put our hands in our mouth, bacteria get into our system. To prevent this, people with cystic fibrosis wash their hands carefully and often with warm soapy water or a hand gel. As well as all the regular immunizations, they must also get shots every year to stop them from getting the flu or pneumonia. They also try to avoid friends who have infectious illnesses until those friends have recovered.

Cross-Infection

People who have life-changing conditions often like to meet or form face-to-face support groups where they can talk to each other, offer advice, and share experiences. This is not possible for cystic fibrosis sufferers. People with cystic fibrosis can never meet each other, because each one has bacteria in their lungs that could be harmful to another. These bacteria grow in the lungs and are usually harmless to people who don't have the condition. But they can be easily passed from one person with cystic fibrosis to another, and they can be very harmful. This is known as cross-infection. It is such a serious risk that at conferences and other meetings about the condition, only one person with cystic fibrosis can be present at a time.

Growing Up

Today there are better treatments for cystic fibrosis sufferers, so people with the condition are living longer than they did in the past. Longer lives, though, bring different challenges for people with cystic fibrosis. As children grow up, they must learn to take responsibility for their own care and treatment. This helps them manage their condition when they go to college, get a job, and move away from home.

More than half of all adults who have cystic fibrosis go to college, get a job, or do the other things they want to in their lives, despite the challenges they face.

Digestive Problems

When children are little, they don't tend to worry if they have gas or problems such as diarrhea and constipation. Digestive problems like these can be embarrassing and more annoying to deal with as children get older, when they are at school, or when they go out with friends. But if they explain the reasons for their problems, most people are understanding, and good friends won't make a big deal of these things.

Having Families

Almost all men who have cystic fibrosis are infertile. This means they cannot have their own children. Some men with cystic fibrosis may adopt children with their partners or they may have surgery or a special fertility treatment. This can sometimes help them to have their own child. Most women who have cystic fibrosis can become pregnant without any problems. The difficulty for women is that being pregnant can make their symptoms worse. There is also the issue of passing on the gene for cystic fibrosis. If someone has cystic fibrosis, that means they have two defective copies of the CFTR gene and will pass one of those on to their child. The baby will either be a carrier or have the condition themselves, depending on the gene they get from the other parent. Some couples choose to have genetic testing to find out if the other partner is a carrier of the CFTR gene. This helps them make a decision about having children together.

Increasing Difficulties

Cystic fibrosis tends to get worse over time. As people with cystic fibrosis get older, their symptoms change and worsen. They may need to take more or different medications, and alter the physical therapy exercises they do or the other treatments they have. For example, people with cystic fibrosis are more likely to get a condition called osteoporosis, which is a thinning of the bones. When cystic fibrosis sufferers have osteoporosis, they may no longer be able to have percussion treatments because it might break their bones. As people get older, the effects of cystic fibrosis start to take their toll and people get weaker. Sadly, most do not live as long as those without the condition.

Chapter 6

Cystic Fibrosis and Gene Therapy

People with cystic fibrosis can face a lifetime of medication and physical therapy to keep their symptoms at bay, so they can lead normal lives. However, in the near future, new techniques may be available to treat the mutations in the CFTR gene in patients with the disorder. This could help their cells be able to make the CFTR protein properly and produce normal mucus. The new treatments are termed gene therapy.

Scientists distinguish between genes using techniques that display the coding chemicals in DNA as bands of different thickness and position.

Gene Therapy

When an automobile is not working, a mechanic may remove and replace the faulty part so it works again. The general idea of gene therapy is similar. Scientists find the section of DNA forming a gene that is not functioning properly and replace it with a new, functioning gene. Gene therapy was first developed in the 1970s. However, it is only in recent times that better laboratory techniques and improved equipment, such as powerful computers, have become available for scientists to use. Using these tools, scientists have so far identified around twenty-one thousand genes in humans, each with a different job to do on its own or in combination with other genes. They have a better idea than ever before of where they need to make gene changes on chromosomes to improve human health. Gene therapy has already been successful in treating some conditions.

Gene Genies

In 2017, scientists successfully used a technique called CRISPR/Cas9 to edit mutations that were causing a rare heart disease. They took sperm donated by a man who had the heart disease and used it to fertilize eggs donated by a woman without the disease in glass containers in a laboratory, producing embryos. Without editing, about half of the embryos had the mutant gene. But after using CRISPR/Cas9 to edit the DNA in the sperm, 72 percent of embryos did not have the mutation causing the disease.

Gene Editing

When an essay has spelling mistakes or parts that don't make sense, we edit and correct it. One type of gene therapy is called gene editing because it uses special techniques to edit and correct the faulty coding in DNA. The main technique, called CRISPR/Cas9, uses a tiny piece of DNA with a chemical code that matches that of the section of DNA sequence that needs to be edited. It binds to this section so that a protein called Cas9, which acts like scissors, can cut out exactly the right part. Then scientists can cut, paste, and delete single letters of the code to make corrections.

Delivering Genes

In gene therapy, the challenge is to get new genes into tiny cells. Scientist have two main ways of delivering new genes to replace mutated genes. One is through the air and the other uses unusual messengers—viruses!

Virus Messengers

If you have ever had a cold, then you have been attacked by a virus. Viruses are incredibly small living things, much smaller even than bacteria, which can only reproduce once they enter a living cell. Once inside, they use energy from this host cell to make hundreds of thousands of copies of their DNA.

Scientists use modified, or changed, viruses as a gene delivery service. In a laboratory, they remove any of the virus's own genes that can cause sicknesses in people. They then replace them with the normal functioning gene to be added in the gene therapy procedure. Viruses enter cells with the mutated version of the gene. The normal gene from the virus "infects" the cell, replacing the mutated gene. The next step of gene therapy is to put cells with the normal gene back into the person with the condition, ideally in places where the tissue needs a helping hand. In someone with cystic fibrosis, for example, large numbers of new cells can be injected into the pancreas or intestinal wall to replace faulty genes and spread copies of the normal gene.

Specialized protein knobs on a virus latch onto particular proteins on the outer surfaces of the cells they target.

Inhaling Genes

In people with lung problems caused by cystic fibrosis, an alternative way of delivering genes is by inhaling them with a nebulizer. In this gene therapy, normal CFTR DNA is encased in bubbles of fat. These bubbles travel to the lungs and deliver the DNA into cells there. In 2015, a trial tested this nebulizer delivery system. It found that when patients used this therapy monthly for a year, they had improved spirometry results and fewer lung infections than those who didn't.

GENE STORIES

"Life changed amazingly pretty soon after I started my nebulizer trial. Within a month of the first dose, I could clear my lungs better, and now I have so much more energy than before. I can go for walks with my family and do PE without getting winded, and I can concentrate so much more easily at school. Gene therapy rocks!"

—*Aaron, age twelve*

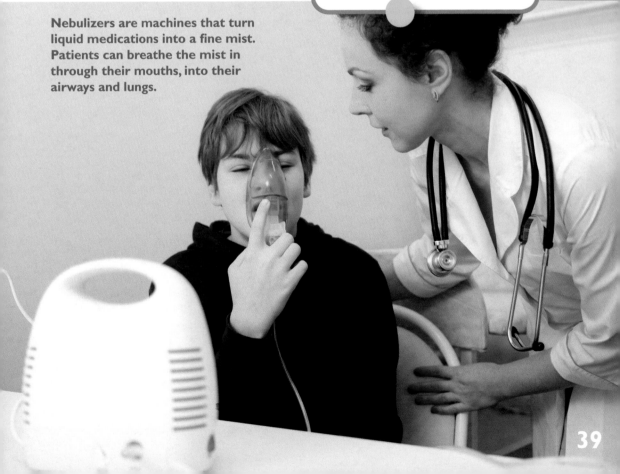

Nebulizers are machines that turn liquid medications into a fine mist. Patients can breathe the mist in through their mouths, into their airways and lungs.

The Challenges of Gene Therapy

Scientists, universities, drug companies, and charities for a variety of inherited diseases have spent billions of dollars globally trying to perfect gene therapy. However, only a few safe, approved therapies are actually currently available. The development process is slow because of the many challenges involved with introducing new genes into cells to keep them working.

Beating the Defenses

A major challenge to gene therapy is the body's immune system, which acts like a defensive shield. This system rallies white blood cells to defend other cells in the body when they detect attack by invaders such as bacteria and viruses. Injected cells containing viruses may be recognized as intruders, too. This immune response can tire people and even make them seriously sick. Doctors sometimes give patients drugs to suppress their immune system to make gene therapy more effective, although this increases a patient's risk of getting an infection.

Gene Delivery

Replacement genes should ideally integrate, or stitch themselves, into DNA on chromosomes in cells. If the gene somehow integrates to the wrong place on chromosomes, or in the wrong tissues, it might cause health problems for patients. For example, in the early twenty-first century, gene therapy for a rare immune disease caused blood cancer in some patients. The introduced genes had changed a gene controlling the growth speed of cells.

Testing on Animals

When a new drug or therapy is developed, it is generally tested first on tissue cultures, but also on animals in laboratories. Scientists usually simulate a human disorder or illness in the animals, then test therapies. But this approach cannot work with some animals. For example, if scientists introduce mutated CFTR genes into mice to give them cystic fibrosis, the mice do not get lung disease. However, pigs can get lung disease with cystic fibrosis, so they are better test animals than mice.

Gene Genies

In 2016, researchers in the United States developed two new virus delivery systems for getting functioning CFTR into the lungs of pigs with cystic fibrosis. One used a type of virus called a lentivirus which directly integrates the CFTR into lung cells, making the change permanent. The other used different viruses, called AAV, that are easier to make in large quantities and specifically target airway cells, but cannot deliver long-lasting effects. Both gene therapies restored normal salt movement in pig airway cells. They also improved the ability of mucus to fight off bacterial infections.

Pig lungs are similar to human lungs, so they can be used in tests to develop safe therapies for cystic fibrosis.

Why Is Gene Therapy Controversial?

Gene therapy interferes with nature and makes changes to the body's set of basic instructions. For these reasons and others, it raises many ethical concerns.

Only for the Rich

Gene therapy is very expensive because it tends to be used on small numbers of people with rare disorders. It can also take years of patient work in laboratories and testing before therapies are safe enough to go on sale. Some people fear this means such expensive therapies will only be available for wealthy people, not everyone.

When developing medical treatments, the cost must be balanced against the number of people likely to benefit from and pay for the therapy.

Designer People

In the future, gene therapies may make it possible to correct many types of mutations in people. For example, they might "fix" sex cells so that replacement, improved genes can be passed on to children, and from those children to their children. This could spare future generations from having diseases such as cystic fibrosis. However, it also might affect how fetuses develop and bring on unexpected health problems. Also, some parents might want to start specifying other gene changes, such as making their children smarter or better at sports. Who decides what traits are good or bad, and what makes a person normal and what makes them disabled? Will society be less accepting of people who are different?

In the future, could technology help people to custom-build babies with fewer health problems? And, if it does, should we allow this?

Use of Stem Cells

Unspecialized cells called stem cells can develop into other distinct types, such as neurons, lung cells, or muscle cells, and can also make multiple copies of themselves. One stem cell can split over and over to produce millions of cells in a body. The stem cells used for cystic fibrosis therapies usually come from bones or blood. But some stem cells come from spare, unused human embryos donated for research by the parents. Some people believe strongly that it is ethically wrong to use these types of cells for gene therapy.

Animal Testing

Many physicians and scientists argue that using animals for testing is necessary. Gene therapies may harm the animals in laboratories, yet many believe this is far better than risking harm to people. Some people, however, have a major problem with harming other living things for the benefit of humans. They also argue that what works in one type of animal will not always work in people, because of their differences.

Hope for the Future

Cystic fibrosis is a very serious disorder that once was severely life limiting. In the past, people with cystic fibrosis would be lucky to live past five years old. Today, there are many more adults than children with cystic fibrosis. As a result of improved medical treatment, nutrition, physical therapy, and understanding of cystic fibrosis, many people with the condition live to be fifty or older, with a greater quality of life than ever before.

Continued Progress in Gene Therapy

Scientists are getting closer to being able to offer safe, effective gene therapies to people with cystic fibrosis, often by building on established techniques. For example, some virus-based gene therapy

Gene therapy has the promise of further extending and improving the lives of people with faulty CFTR genes.

effectively targets mutated genes, but the changes may not be permanent, so repeat therapy is needed. Additionally, gene editing can be very accurate in the laboratory, but is impractical for targeting cells hidden inside human bodies. The limitations of these two approaches are being dealt with through second-generation gene repair. This therapy combines the gene delivery ability of viruses with the permanent gene-editing abilities of CRISPR/Cas9. The promise of second-generation gene repair is that it can permanently correct the region of chromosome 7 containing the six most common CFTR mutations. These include Delta F508, and around 80 percent of the less-common mutations in people with cystic fibrosis.

GENE STORIES

"The future is suddenly looking a whole lot brighter with the advent [approach] of precision medicines and gene therapy around the corner. There is now real hope that I, and people like me, can experience a life without the shadow of sickness."
—Stefan, age thirty

Personalized Health Care

In the near future, people with different cystic fibrosis variants will have access to different types of personalized health care. This will help them cope with their particular symptoms. Many therapies for cystic fibrosis treat general symptoms such as lung infection or lack of pancreatic enzymes. However, precision medicines directly target the causes of cystic fibrosis associated with particular variants. In these, chemicals interact with the faulty CFTR protein to make it work better. For example, ivacaftor helps to open gates in cell membranes to let salt move more effectively. Gate mutations affect less than 10 percent of people with cystic fibrosis, so there is no point giving this medication to others who do not have such mutations. Another drug, lumacaftor, helps get more CFTR protein to the surface of cells, and is more suitable to people with other variants.

Glossary

amino acids Substances that help the body build proteins.

antibiotics Medicines that kill bacteria.

asthma Disease that causes breathlessness and wheezing.

bacteria Tiny living things that can cause disease.

cancer A disease caused by the abnormal growth of body cells.

carriers People who can pass on a condition but do not have the symptoms of it themselves.

cells Basic building blocks of all living things.

chromosomes Parts of a cell that contain the genes which control how we grow and if we are born male or female.

cilia Tiny, hairlike parts on cells.

constipated Unable to pass stools, or solid waste.

descendants People in later generations related to a person, with shared genes.

dieticians Health care workers who help people eat healthily.

digestive system The system that processes food to extract nutrients for the body.

DNA A protein that contains the instructions an organism needs to develop, live, and reproduce.

donor Someone who donates or gives something.

eggs Female reproductive cells.

embryo A human in the early stages of development before it is born.

enzymes Substances that help to cause natural processes, such as digestion, in animals and plants.

esophagus Tube that leads from the mouth through the throat to the stomach.

exhaling Breathing out.

fetus A human in the later stages of development before it is born.

fiber Substance found in plant foods that cannot be digested but that helps people to digest other food.

genes Parts of a cell that control or influence the way a person looks, grows, and develops.

human genome All the genetic information in a person.

immune system Body parts that work together to protect the body against disease.

infections Kinds of diseases that can be caught from other people.

intestines Tubes through which food passes when it has left the stomach.

lungs Two organs that people and animals use to breathe air.

membranes Thin layers that surround and cover cells.

mucus A thick, slimy substance that is produced by the lining of some organs of the body.

mutations Significant changes in the structure of a gene.

nutrients Substances found in food that help humans and other animals to be healthy.

organs Body parts with specific functions, such as the heart and the brain.

pancreas A part of the body that releases digestive enzymes into the blood.

pelvic floor Muscle layer that supports the bladder, uterus, and bowel, and closes the bladder outlet and back passage.

physical therapy Treatment using movement and exercise that helps people who are sick.

protein A substance that does most of the work in cells and is required for the structure, function, and regulation of the body's tissues and organs.

radiation A type of energy.

reproduce Produce offspring.

respiratory system The body parts that take in oxygen and release carbon dioxide.

species Type of living thing.

sperm Male reproductive cells.

spirometer A machine that measures how much air lungs can hold.

stem cells Types of cells that can divide to produce not only more stem cells but also cells that can turn into many different types of cells.

symptoms Changes in the body or mind caused by a disease or health condition.

tissues Large masses of similar cells that make up a part of an organism and perform a specific function, such as skin or muscle tissue.

transplant To transfer an organ or tissue from one individual to another.

viruses Tiny organisms that invade and live in body cells and cause disease.

For Further Reading

Abramovitz, Melissa. *Cystic Fibrosis.* Detroit, MI: Lucent Books, 2013.

Anders, Mason. *Heredity.* North Mankato, MN: Capstone Press, 2018.

Hawkins, Carole. *Asthma, Cystic Fibrosis, and Other Respiratory Disorders.* Broomall, PA: Mason Crest, 2018

Miller, Petra. *Cystic Fibrosis.* New York, NY: Cavendish Square, 2016.

Mooney, Carla. *Genetics: Breaking the Code of Your DNA.* White River Junction, VT: Nomad Press, 2014.

Powell, Jillian. *Explaining Cystic Fibrosis.* Mankato, MN: Smart Apple Media, 2010.

Index